THE LITTLE BOOK OF
CORGI CHARM

Words of cheer from the world's smiliest dog

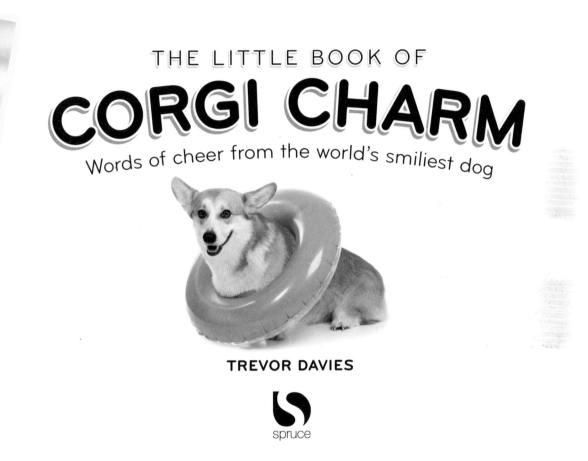

THE LITTLE BOOK OF
CORGI CHARM

Words of cheer from the world's smiliest dog

TREVOR DAVIES

spruce

An Hachette UK Company
www.hachette.co.uk

First published in Great Britain in 2014 by
Spruce, a division of Octopus Publishing Group Ltd
Endeavour House
189 Shaftesbury Avenue
London
WC2H 8JY
www.octopusbooks.co.uk
www.octopusbooksusa.com

Distributed in the US by
Hachette Book Group USA
237 Park Avenue
New York NY 10017 USA

Distributed in Canada by
Canadian Manda Group
664 Annette Street
Toronto, Ontario, Canada M6S 2C8

Trevor Davies asserts the moral right to be identified as the author
of this work

ISBN 978-1-84601-476-5

A CIP catalogue record for this book is available from the British Library

Printed and bound in China

Picture Acknowledgments

123RF Svetlana Pisareva 61. age footstock eriklam 77. Alamy amana
images inc. 2 above right, 24, 31; Barbara von Hoffmann 16. Ardea
John Daniels 76. CanStockPhoto p_marks 26. Corbis Andrew Grant 52;
Mark Raycroft/Minden Pictures 21, 33; Naho Yoshizawa/Aflo 9 above
left, 15, 23, 41 below left. Fotolia Julia Remezova 17. Getty Images 14;
Bryant Scannell 2 below right, 45; Catherine Ledner 67; David Samuel
Robbins 4, 49; Dawn D. Hanna 8, 12, 55 below right, 56; Holly Hildreth 6,
7, 13, 22, 28, 41 above left, 41 above right, 43, 46, 51, 62, 65 left, 69, 78,
79; Jajauma Corgis 40, 44; Jim Richardson 74; Lon Fong Martin 5 below
left, 65 right, 71; Marc Dalangin 25 below right, 54, 59; Mark Raycroft/
Minden Pictures 34, 57, 64, 70; moaan 5 above, 9 above centre, 10, 55
above right, 58; Photo by Marcelo Maia 19; Photographed by Sheed 18;
Purple Collar Pet Photography 1, 2 left, 29, 32, 36; Sarah L. Voisin/The
Washington Post via Getty Images 9 above right, 11, 41 centre; Terry J
Alcorn 9 below left, 20, 68; Tim Graham 50. Glow Images Heather Perry
27; Jakob Helbig 80; Naho Yoshizawa/Aflo 53; SuperStock 30, 55 above
left, 63; Yosuke Tanaka/Aflo 4 below, 42. Krispy Krumb 47. Shutterstock
HelenaQueen 3, 73. SuperStock Corbis 60; Minden Pictures 25 centre,
38; Randi Hirschmann/Science Faction 25 below left, 35. Thinkstock Big
Cheese Photo 25 above left, 37; Elena Rakhuba/iStock 39; HelenaQueen/
iStock 48, 72; Sergey Lavrentev/iStock 5 above left, 65 centre, 66.
Warren Photographic 75.

CONTENTS

INTRODUCTION

It was the divine Siddhartha Gautama who once said, 'No one saves us but ourselves. No one can and no one may. We ourselves must walk the path. Although if we took a Corgi on this walk, we'd have more giggles.' Aristotle taught us that 'love is a single soul inhabiting two bodies and a short, smiley dog'. Confucius, he say, 'Corgis are cool.' So, from these minor misquotes you can see that the wisest men in history have understood the nurturing powers of these waggy little Welsh wizards.

The truth is that corgis are on to something, some divine secret of happiness that man has yet to fathom. We don't know its nature, but we're pretty sure it's something impressive. Just look at their faces – those challenging eyes, that big smiley mouth. And that stature! Only 12 inches tall, but a mile high in pride. It's no surprise that

monarchs trust them as their confidants and that pixies ride them into battle (in the Great Pixie War of 1820, no less than 100 Pembrokes were mobilized, as depicted in the harrowing film *War Corgi*).

Several animals have tried to usurp the corgi mantle of the world's happiest animal – kittens with their playful antics and huggable cuteness; penguins with their knock-about visual humour and patented silly walk; red pandas, which look as if they were created by a nine-year-old girl – but none have quite got life as sussed as the Corgi.

There are two flavours of Corgi: Pembroke and Cardigan. Scientists have yet to work out which is happier. It's possibly as futile as trying to work out which river is the wettest or which of your legs is your favourite. Both breeds have that knowing look of a companion who understands exactly what it takes to make you smile, so whichever variety you're faced with, be assured you're in safe paws and will be charmed by their contagious happiness within seconds.

In this book I'm not trying to open a window on the Corgi's psyche, more trying to harness its powers for greater human good, a kind of canine therapy for the dogless. This dog can nourish the soul, teach us to love, end world conflict and, most of all, have fun. So why not take in a Corgi a day. Try one for when you're feeling low; one for when you're lonely; one for inspiration, aspiration and guidance along life's precarious path.

So read on, heed their advice and learn their lessons and you too can reach enlightenment, be charmed and as happy as a Corgi.

Corgis for
the Soul

Find Your Place in the Sun

Harriet regretted bringing the family here. She hadn't realized it was 'that' kind of beach, nor that her husband would be so keen to join in.

Love Your Country

Hank 'Apple-pie-born-on-the-Fourth-of-July' Jackson was excited ahead of his attempt to 'play catch' at the Superbowl.

Act Like a Princess

Celia's tiara was a touch snug, but if anyone could pull it off...

Perfect the Art of Seduction

'Underneath all this fur I'm naked.'

Enjoy Time With the Family

As the tide came in, Monty wondered whether he'd been a touch over-zealous when playing with the kids.

Embrace the Day

'Morning world, today will be the day I bench press 180lbs, start my memoirs, ask for a raise and propose to Meredith ... or I could just kick back and watch the shopping channel all day.'

Cultivate Your Garden

'I plant the seed.
Nature grows the seed.
I poo on the seed and dig up
all the surrounding seeds.'

Enjoy Something From Your Youth

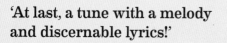

'At last, a tune with a melody and discernable lyrics!'

Make Yourself Laugh

Finally, Dave had found someone to pull his finger.

Pig Out!

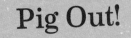

Delia would remember that first dates shouldn't end up with you falling asleep in your food.

Style It Out

Derek 'did' summer like no other Corgi.

'Seriously boys, judging by all those beach babes, this is going to be one hell of a holiday.'

Concentrate on the Good Times

The smell of the new carpet had put Crackers right off his game.

Pamper Yourself

'I borrowed your credit card and got a pedicure... what d'ya think?'

Corgis for Inspiration

Terry was only the third Corgi ever to conquer the Dooglehorn, and the first to do so drunk.

'It's a bit choppy to be sunbathing on the stern, Daphne... Daphne?'

Do something impulsive

'Penelope, would you do me the great honour of... putting my mother's ring on eBay? I'm trying to save up for a new TV.'

'I'll give you a clue to where I buried your wallet... somewhere sandy.'

Plant Something

It was their first attempt at gardening, and Digby and Teasle soon discovered why they call them 'containers'.

WOODEN BOX
WE LOVE NATURAL

Hang Out With Your Bestest Buddy

Zak and his wingman Eddie were the founder members of the Westside White Paw Gang.

Go for a Thrill Ride

Colin couldn't drive, but he'd let the handbrake off and was loving the buzz.

Impress Your Friends

'I will now proceed to push the Great Suprendo over the falls!'

Hit the Slopes

'Seriously, buddy, if you can't make this thing go faster, let's just give up, go inside and get blasted on eggnog.'

Go for a Drive in the Country

'Don't worry about the colour, Barney, all the ladies love a convertible.'

'I'm not dragging you out again if your sorry ass can't make the pontoon.'

Boyd had found Penny's make-up and stumbled upon an edgier look.

Have a Stab at Heroism

Having volunteered to save the cat from the tree, Dexter realized he was in a remarkably similar situation.

Dave found nothing lifted his spirits quite like a little rustle in the panty drawer.

Corgis
for Calm

Try a Change of Scene

Kenneth and Agnes pose for the cover of *Country Corgi Cribs*.

Find Your Inner Puppy

The will was strong, but the legs were short.

She had chanted mantras.
She had meditated with yogis.
But she eventually achieved a supreme
state of inner peace via Pinot Grigio.

While the boss sorted the drinks,
Chips settled down to watch the game.

Go on Holiday

'You threw a what in the what?'

Seek Out Like-Minded Company

At the Corgis For Justice AGM, Ernie was voted in as Treasurer and the motion to defecate in next-door's containers was carried.

Face it Out

Dr Seuss's Corgi dreaded turning up at funerals.

Believe Your Dreams Can Come True

As first dates go, this was shaping up pretty well. All Carter wanted now was a cloud slipper and a cloud lamppost.

'She angry with you too, huh?'

Find a Safe Place

Only Mr Snuffles understood Tyson.

Seek an
Alternative
Way to
De-Stress

Look into my eyes... relax...
Harvey the Hypnohound will
banish your fears for a remarkably
reasonable hourly rate.

Take a Power Nap

Sigmund dreamt of guitars, wine, women and cars... but mostly he dreamt about having longer legs.

Corgis for
Wisdom

Never Look Back

Basil couldn't believe it was only 273 days until Christmas.

In his eagerness to collect
wood for the burner,
Hobnob had inadvertently
ended up in Scandinavia.

Embrace the Seasons

Like the sunset on a crisp winter evening,
Like the cherry blossom in spring.

Or a warm autumn breeze...
That's what sausages mean to me.

Enjoy
Recuperation

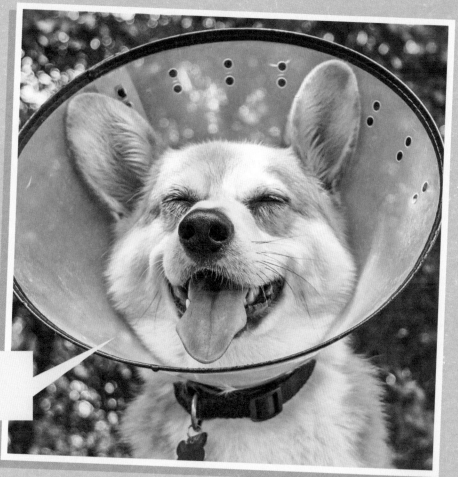

'Plug me into the TV and let's see what we pick up!'

Never Give Up on Your Dreams

Despite being told countless times that he wasn't a horse, Buster would never give up on his Olympic show-jumping ambitions.

Try an Intellectual Challenge

'Sorry, I was protecting my Queen. It's what us Corgis do.'

Challenge What's Accepted

Duncan didn't know whether Hamlet had a dog, but he thought he'd audition anyway.

Revel in Your Chores

After three hours' looking, they finally conceded they'd never find that missing sock.

Corgis for Self-Improvement

Never Give Up

Riley was winning this battle in the eternal struggle of winter vs short dogs.

Surprise Your Partner

Following a disastrous experiment with cubism, Bernard entered his blue period.

Celebrate a Saint's Day

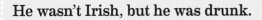

He wasn't Irish, but he was drunk.

Although he wasn't, strictly speaking, a 'qualified' surgeon, Barry had read a lot of books and wondered how hard a hip replacement could be?

Be Generous

'If we keep smiling, Archie, they may not notice the missing ham.'

Share Something Precious

'I know it's not much, my darling, but I nearly got kicked out of Wimbledon getting you this.'

Make Someone Feel Good About Themselves

'Honestly, I love it, darling.
It will go perfectly with the
balaclava you gave me last year.'

Surprise Yourself

It was either aqua aerobics or cheesecake this evening, and, against all expectations, Beryl chose the former.

François took questions from the press ahead of his attempt to become the first Corgi to clear 20 restaurant tables on a unicycle.

Share
Something
Personal

'You see... completely gone! That's the last time I go for walkies to the vet.'

Try a New Look

Constance's new hat made her feel special somehow.

'What say you and me team up and rid the streets of crime forever? You be the brains, I'll be the muscle.'

Find
Your
Soulmate

DOGS2DOGS
Full name: Winston C. Starbuck
Fruitmachine Jnr
Pet name: Jiffy
Likes: Barking at cars, digging in
daffodils and scraps
WLTM: Short-legged, like-
minded non-smoker for chasing
squirrels, maybe more.

Harold felt that flowers weren't enough of an apology... to win her back, he'd have to go a step further.

Plan Ahead

Toby regretted filling up on bread rolls before the main course.